Poetic Culture Vol. 1

By CarolinaKiddDaPoet

Cover Created by Jazzy Kitty Publications

Poetic Culture Logo by Isaac Brown III

Logo Designs by Andre M. Saunders/Leroy Grayson

Editor: Anelda Attaway

© 2021 Isaac Ray Brown Jr.

ISBN 978-1-954425-20-0

Library of Congress Control Number: 2021904487

All rights reserved. This book is protected by the copyright laws of the United States of America. This book may not be copied or reprinted for commercial gain or profit. The use of short quotations or occasional page copying for personal or group study is permitted and encouraged. Permission will be granted upon request. For Worldwide Distribution. Printed in the United States of America. Published by Jazzy Kitty Publications utilizing Microsoft Publishing Software and Bookcover Pro. The Holy Scriptures are from the Holy Bible.

DEDICATIONS

I dedicate this book of poems to my late mother Tammy Wiggins Brown. The strongest woman to ever live.

ACKNOWLEDMENTS

The only being I want to acknowledge is my Lord, God. For He is so worthy, and I am undeserving of His mercy and grace. If not for You Lord, where would I be?

Thank You for Your wisdom, Your guidance, and Your strength for me to lean on Lord. I know as long as I keep You first it will always work out for my greater good.

Amen.

TABLE OF CONTENTS

Introduction	i
A Love Affair	02
americA	10
Average Day in the Hood	18
Cain & Abel	26
Choices	33
Compass	36
Count Meltdown	39
Crazy Thoughts	42
Drunk Dial	48
Edification	53
Encouraging Words	57
Fallen Leaf	64
Geometry	67
Love Poem	73
Masquerade	84
My Addiction	87
On My Mind	91
Reminiscing	95
Role Model Father	99
Same Ole Story	107
Silver Lining	110
Subconscious	115

TABLE OF CONTENTS

The difference between me and you.. 120

Tomorrow.. 123

Trial & Error... 126

Trust the Process.. 129

Uprooted Against My Will... 136

What She Can't Have 140

Zurita Murphy.. 145

About the Author.. 148

INTRODUCTION

The name Poetic Culture came about through brainstorming with a co-worker late one night on the job as we passed the time on third shift. We shuffled through a few titles and finally reached a consensus on the title presented before you today.

Poetic Culture is a book of poems that I hope will touch others' spirit and soul how it has blessed mine. There are so many relatable pieces within this book for you to discover. It is filled with sex, loyalty, happiness, pain, encouragement, and history. All of your emotions will cycle in and out of your heart and mind. This edition is long overdue, and my own procrastination is the only reason why instead of you as the reader reading Volume 1, aren't reading at least Volume 4 of Poetic Culture by now.

Poetry, I do believe, is my calling card, my safe haven, my niche, and my talent. God blessed me with the gift of gab, as some would say. Seriously though, He has blessed me with a gift of creativity that allows me to form words on paper that mend and blend with rhyme and all kinds of reasons. So, sit back, relax, and indulge in letters that make words form sentences into paragraphs.

A Love Affair

BUT NOW YOU'VE ENCOURAGED ME
TO COME OVER
LIKE A GAME OF RED ROVER!
I'M FEELING LUCKIER THAN AN IRISHMAN
WITH A FOUR-LEAF CLOVER

Poetic Culture Vol. 1
A Love Affair

It's 2 a.m.

And you hit my Phone!

Supplying me with Vital Information

Bout ya man NEVER being Home

He's always Gone

Never right

But left you feeling Wrong

And Alone!

Going on some weeks now

You've been Playing me this same Sad Song.

But now you've Encouraged me to Come Over.

Like a game of Red Rover!

I'm feeling Luckier than an Irishman

With a Four-Leaf Clover

So now I make Provision

For this intimate Collision.

And to think it all started

From the Moment that I Listened.

I approached your Doorstep
That's where it all Begins
But this **Love Affair** started
Before you prompted me to Come in

Sit down, have a Drink.
I notice you're Horny and Emotional
So I think
I'ma take Full Advantage
Granted!

That's what you wanted me to do!

Be the Pilot to your Private
Leave you Lost for Words
I'm talking Sex Face Silent.

Aggressively you snatch off my Clothes
Seductively you De Robe
Next, I touch your Soul,
Reaching G-spot Goals
We both in here Playing House
I mean the Wife and Hubby Role

I know we both have a Significant Other
But now the only thing I'm tryna Discover
Is the seam between the Bed and the Cover
I'm talking so close
The only Intervention is a Latex Rubber.

Right now, you are Mine
We are One
Baby, I'm Not Finished
Until you're Done.

Sex like this
We might go half on a baby girl or a son
Why is it that things so Wrong
Are always the Most Fun

I mean, it Tastes Better
Feel Wetter
Ass softer than Quill Feathers
Man, that's Soft!

Our secrets run deeper than Randy Moss,
And our dirty past made a Filthy Future
Yea, we really got too much Sauce.

No cares

For these Continuous **Love Affairs**

But both Parties Remain Unaware

Of our Eager Lust

Falling into **Dangerous Love**,

But warning comes before Destruction

So instead of following simple

Love Affair Instructions

We lose our heads

Mental reduction

Abuse Our Hearts

Emotional Corruption

And that's where things Get Messy

When you address me

So Sexy

Saying Daddy, Please just caress me!

Your wish becomes My Command

And I'm starting to understand

That My Desire

Is the Igniter to your Fire

Yes, I long to be the Rim

To your Firestone Tire.

I'm truly admired

So whatever it Requires

In this **Love Affair** to Acquire

I'm with it

Every day our Sinful Acts Travel

But you cause Mine to Pivot

You paint a picture so Vivid

Of False Hope

If we Lived it

Upon my Hands

Your Every Word is Encrypted

Because I Cling to your Breath

Until NO AIR is Left

Suffocation!

Sick the moment we Depart

Your deadly Medication!

My I.Q. Level Diminishing

Deterioration of Education!

Well!

At least that's how I feel,

But this was supposed to be a Fling

Falling in Love was NEVER Part of the Deal

So let me get back to what's Really Real

And go Back Home to Mine

Physically my Body is there

But I left My Mind.

It's still Trapped about an Hour Ago

In the Past Time.

But again, I Promise myself

That **Love Affair** was the Last Time

Yet REPETITIVELY, I catch myself

REPEATING THAT LAST LINE.

On God, I'm trying
Because between Him, My Lady, and Myself
Is where I CONSISTENTLY keep Lying
Causing my Relationship to Decline
Instead of Incline

In other words, the Rewind
Delays the Fast Forward Motion
Recycling Negative Drama
Relationship Erosion!

That's what Eats Us Apart.
What is now Bad Intentions
Was Good Vibes from the Start

I'm not Comprehending
But somehow, we MISSED OUR MARK!

And that's what lead me
To This Love Affair

americA

BUT WHAT'S THE POINT OF WINNING BATTLES
IN A DEAD-END ENDLESS WAR
GEORGE FLOYD WAS JUST BURIED
WHAT DID DR. KING DIE FOR?

americA

The Sirens Loud
But the Lights are Louder
Blue to Red lights
Headlights, Flashlights
Cop in All-Black
But his face Pale White

My View
In his Sight
Went Left
That AIN'T Right.

Just being Black
In any form
Makes me a Stereotype

We are a Minority
Amongst the Majority
For too many years

We put up with

Unjust Authorities

And us Brothers

Need our Sisters Front Lining

Like Sororities

Black Queens, we need you.

Their Killing your sons

Black Queens, we Bleed you

But what's the point of Winning Battles

In a Dead-end Endless War

George Floyd was just Buried

What did Dr. King die for?

It really Hurts to the Core

America's Racism at a Standstill

Racist mines all over the Landfill

CAREFUL WATCH YOUR STEP!

If you're not your Brother's Keeper

Grim Reaper Ole have 'em kept

Pushing Flowers as he Slept

John 11:35 like Jesus
Boy I Wept

And Yes, I continue to Weep
And Yes, I continue to Lose Sleep
Cause Yes, we continue to get Beat
And Yes, it's in our Own Streets.

How should I Train My Boys
To deal with Cops
Once they're Stopped

On a random Friday Evening
Head on Concrete
Lungs Barely Breathing
Blood Steady Leaking
My son really Bleeding

Mouth on the Pavement
Like a Baby when he Teething
Just for being Black in **americA**

Only Reason

Yea, times have Changed

But I treat it like Seasons

Because as a Nation

We always reach a Cold Place

But we Spring into a Warm Space

But usually, Fall Back

Into those Cold Traits

The Circle of Nature

Is the Cycle of Humanity

How can **americA** change

While providing similar results

That's Insanity

These Stupid Mother. . .

Bout to make me use Profanity

Luckily, I'm Heated

But my Listeners

A Fan of me

Close to the Cross

Hands Folded

Y'all be Praying for me

Drake said it Best

I believe in God's Plan for me

I'm only 28

With a Great Plan AHEAD of Me.

Rainy day on my Parade

George Floyd, May Weather, Me

Stomach feeling Weak

Numbness in my Feet

How can a Heart So Cold

Release the MOST Heat

Clock out with No Remorse

Clock in and Repeat.

I mean, it's really Outta Hand

And running Deeper than Deep

americA,

The Land of the Free,

And the Home of the Brave.

Well, call me Kunta

Cause we still Enslaved

White Man Attack

And we Steal and Raid

Rioting Walmart

Stealing Raid

Amongst others things

But, I get the Big Picture

Riots are the Voice of the Unheard

White **americA,** PLEASE LISTEN

And EVERY DAY we Pay

So, Free Attention

History was NEVER Recorded Correctly

Maybe they just FORGOT to Mention Us

Or maybe they Suffered from Dementia

But Either way,

We must Protest,

We must Program,

We must Progress.

#justiceforBreonnaTaylor

You weren't my Blood Sister

But our Skin Tones Favor

Myles, Brett, Jonathan

Jonathan, Myles, Brett

Repetition, Reminiscing

Making SURE you DON'T Forget

Shout her Name til it's Justified

BREONNA TAYLOR!!!!!!

Shout her Name til it's Rectified

BREONNA TAYLOR!!!!!!

Average Day in the Hood

**KICKING IT WITH THE BOYS.
REMINISCING, JOKING, AND THINKING
MAKING A WHOLE LOT OF NOISE!**

Average Day in the Hood

Cooling, Smoking, Drinking
Kickin' it with the boys.
Reminiscing, Joking, and Thinking
Making a Whole Lot of Noise!

Speaker Blasting, Blunt Passing
The homie says,
"Throw on the Instrumental."
We all go off the Roof
Note Pad with NO Pencil!

As we pass around the Juice
The whole team a Little Loose
Old Lady Hattie bout to Lose it
Banging on the door
Yelling turn down the Music

So, we turn it Down a Level
She shaking her head
She notices our Eyes Low
And Redder than the devil!

Told us she's going back in the House

It's Late

And she and her Spouse

Gotta get to the Cheese in the A.M.

Like a Couple of Mouse

Improper

I meant Mice

Now Niggas talkin' SHIT

I break out the Dice

Fives the Point

It came out Twice

I'm in Niggas heads

As if I were Lice

The Chosen One for this Game

Call me Jesus Christ

The homies mad

But it's all Love

Collect my Earnings

Call up the Plug

I get an 8th

Then we Light up the Drugs.

Now we back on One

But we aren't Close to Done

I run to the Corner Store

And gather up the Party Pack!

I'm talking Rellos, Blacks,

Dollar Juice and Little Debbie Snacks.

Now on the way back to the Crib

The Hood won't let you Live.

Shit, it might be a Loose Pit

Off his Collar

Or Lil Reg

Begging for a Dollar

Hood Hoes everywhere!

If she's cute, I might Holla.

Then it's Back to the Crib

Now the Homies Watching Shottas!

Aw man, what a Classic,

Wayne and the Gang

Walking round like a Savage.

We see it too many times

It's Turned into a Habit.

That Boy Mad Max was Hell!

Dropping Niggas off in Caskets.

Meanwhile, during the Movie

We hear Shots Firing!

Turns out some Young Niggas

Gun downed an Old Head

Coming up on Retirement!

Bout a Whole Hour Spent

Nowhere come the Feds!

Shaking my Head!

This man is Proclaimed Dead.

A body Full of Lead

And he's Covered in Red.

The Hood feels his Pain

So many Tears were Shed,

But when twelve asked what happened

You know Nothing was said!

Total Silence
To the Violence!
Call **the Hood** Hellen Keller

No Vision and it can't hear
Closed eye
With a Covered Ear
Mouths Sealed
Because of Fear.

But back between the Four Walls
We have a Loud Discussion
Wondering if the Young Niggas are caught
What'll be their Repercussion?

But after while, we just drop it
It's an **Average Day in the Hood**
So we just Switch the Topic.

My homie says, he knows a Female
That got a Friend or Two
Or maybe a Few
And they might come Through.

OR MAYBE NOT!

He really be Lying

Bout all the Hoes he got.

I mean, he might got a Thot

Or maybe even Two,

But do you really even Count 'em

If they been Passed Round the Crew?!

But that's a whole nother Topic!

So we switch it up again.

I got another homie

And we all just call him Twin

He said he was Hooping yesterday

Score went to 12, and he had 10,

And before he went

He had 2 Blunts and 3 shots of Jin.

He stays Bragging!

Cocky Nigga,

But he do be Swagging!

Iconic Hood Figure

And he Keeps us Laughing.

But that's an **Average Day in the Hood**

And I'ma Above Average Individual

That's Tryna Do Good!

Tryna 'Do The Right Thing'

Yea, I'm talking Spike Lee

Flow on Pizza Boy Delivery

Now that's. . .a little bit about me.

See now, my last homeboy!

Is truly a Product of his Environment

Has a Past I can't really Speak On

But at least now he's in Retirement

But he do keep some Young Niggas

Trained to go for Hiring.

But that's an **Average Day in the Hood.**

So after a Long Day at Work

Doing what we should

We link up together

To Past Time

Refreshing each other's minds

On what we did the last time

CAUSE THAT'S AN **AVERAGE DAY IN THE HOOD**.

Cain & Abel

THIS STORY IS A TALE OF TWO BROTHERS
THEY HAD A CLOSE BOND
BUT ONE WAS JEALOUS OF THE OTHER

YOU SEE, IN CAIN EYES
HE FELT HE WAS FIRST IN LINE
UNTIL ABEL CAME ALONG
AND THROUGH SHADE ON HIS SHINE.

Cain & Abel

This story is a Tale of Two Brothers
They had a Close Bond
But one was Jealous of the other
He salaciously Desired
After his brothers' Lover!

You see, in **Cain** eyes
He felt he was First-In-Line
Until **Abel** came along
And through Shade on his Shine.

Grabbing all of her Attention,
Her Body and her Mind.
She started a War between them
9/11, and she was the Dime!

Yes, she was Fine
An Extraordinary, Beautiful Concubine!
But NEVER was she Worth the Crime
Not enough Value to Trade your Life in,
TO SERVE THE TIME!

But **Cain** thought she was

His Fatal Love for her

Makes him do what he does.

His Heart Grows Colder

The more he sees them together!

He tells **Abel** to use his Shoulder

When things are Troubling

And NOT getting Any Better.

The definition of a Wolf

In Sheeps Clothing!

Like a naked Delilah

The moment she started Disrobing.

A Beautiful Beast!

Starving for the Naïve

Ready to Feast,

Off his Leash

Cain's thinking Violence

Is the only way to Peace

When she left

She took his Mind

All he got back was a Piece!

So he's NOT Stable

But instead of Blaming her

He puts it all on **Abel**

Watching his Brothers' every move

Like Suddenlink Cable.

He's PAST Determined

Not Listening to Momma,

Grandma,

Or even the Preachers Sermon.

His eyes Clouded by Anger

His Soul Burning with Fire

His Heart Torn

But now Mended

With Envious Desire!

So he Plots,
And he Schemes,
For sure his Love
Will be Redeemed!

Tryna find a way
To bring himself
To his Esteem

Longing to Repair his Pride
Yes, he Prays
But only for the devil
To Remain Inside!

He's after Revenge!
Salivating over the Thoughts
Of his Pre Meditated Sins

Anger with Ambition
Is Uncontrollable
Once it Blends.

A plan with NO Strategy,

Just a Man performing Tragedy.

Intentional Casualties

She told him

Cain maybe one day

But actually

That's Blasphemy!

Making a Mockery

Of his Emotions

Causing a DEADLY

Mental Explosion

Envy, Hatred, & Strife

What a Fatal Mix of Potions

So, **Cain** does the Unthinkable

Committing the Perfect Crime

That doesn't leave him Linkable

Stirred a Chemical Element

In his Wine

Yet, still leaves it Drinkable

Abel's got Arsenic in his Veins!

He's feeling Numb, got Diarrhea,

And bad Abdominal Pains!

A Brother Dead

WHAT A SHAME!

Was it really worth it **Cain**?!?!

All of this, for what?!?!

HER HEART YOU STILL WON'T GAIN!

Choices

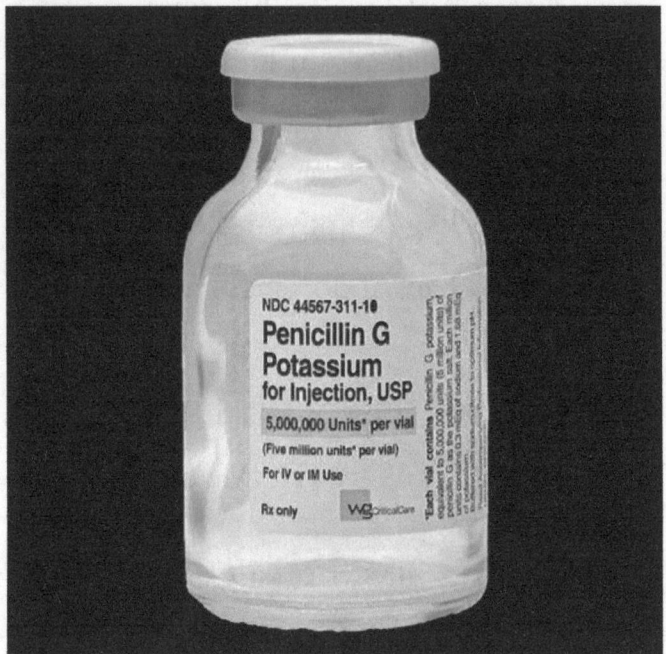

**FACING ANOTHER DECISION
BUT EVERY AVENUE IS INFESTED
INFECTED, NOW I'M AFFECTED
NEED A SHOT OF PENICILLIN!**

Choices

The **Choices** I've made
Keeps me Enslaved
To the Problems that Fade

Into my Existence
Didn't have to be this way
It could've been Okay

But I chose Resistance
Could've made a Difference
Instead, I showed Persistence
In the right thing to do
To keep my Distance.

Now I feel a Major Payne
But homie I AIN'T NO Clown
No Damon Wayne

A lot of Shame
In my Game
A little Ashamed
Of my Name

Man, I sound Broken

Because of choices between Good or Bad

And Evil is what was Chosen

Thinking of making that East to West move

Like Demar Derozen!

But currently, I'm Frozen

Facing another decision

But every avenue is infested

Infected, now I'm affected

Need a Shot of Penicillin!

Lord willing

I can handle my Dealings

Bottle My Feelings

Until they Combust

And I lose all Trust

In my inner me

My Life is Bittersweet

And I can't Blame the Enemy

Cause all he did

Was Provide a Choice!

COMPASS

I'LL FOLLOW MY COMPASS,
UNTIL I'M ACCOMPLISHED

Compass

My **Compass** like Olympus

Has fallen

Loss of Direction

Stuck in the middle Stalling

Head down

On my knees Crawling

Nigga get up

Rise for the Occasion

Exit Procrastination

Our greatest Enemy

On the Mic

My Tongue is the Pen in me

Hard work brings a Profit

Well, what an Epiphany

Me and Loco, no other Partners

We work Independently

No Toy Story Tommy

You won't find a friend in me

Good in Reverse Energy

Consumes my Memory

Damaging my Thoughts

That weren't handled Gingerly

So the only fear in me is Cupid

Multiple Rerun Episodes

Of her making me Look Stupid

Shooting Flirtatious Darts

As if I know how to use it

But the Dummy in me

Won't let me Refuse it

So. . .here we go

Something else to settle fo

We bicker Back and Forth

The Teapot and Kettle show

Forbidden skeletons

From places, we promised we wouldn't go

Heavens yes or Hell no

East to West

Through Hail or Snow

I'll follow my **Compass,**

Until I'm Accomplished.

So Deal with it Nigga

We in the Field with it Nigga

Consequences for anyone

Who Interferes with it Nigga

A lost Soul

Is outta Control

Weak Minded

Easy to Mold

Like Clothes

Easy to Fold

Fall for a Shiny

Fool's Gold

So who knows

The Road

From which you chose

My Goals, My Destinations

I won't forget those

But it all starts

With My COMPASS.

Count Meltdown

20 years later

Still suffering from COVID-19

With an 18-year-old

Who made him a Grandfather

By the age of 17

After a Miscarriage and Abortion

By the age of 16

15 minutes after realizing

That this Lifestyle must be her Fate

She went through about 14 seasons

With 13 reasons why 12 NEVER Rescued her

11 times she's been Molested

Before the age of 10

Her Paranoia keeps a 9 on her side

Cause after 8 the sun goes down

And it WON'T STOP

Like 7 Streeter

6 Months

5 days in Rehab

And she's still looking 4 a Change

She was prescribed 3 different Medications

A Sunday, Monday, and 2's day pill

She's 1 unhappy woman

With Zero Confidence amongst herself

CarolinaKiddDaPoet
Crazy Thoughts

**THE BIBLE SAYS
AN IDLE MIND
IS THE DEVILS WORKSHOP**

Crazy Thoughts

The Bible says

An Idle Mind

Is the devils' workshop

So when I'm alone

I better stop thinking So Long

Cause the 1st person I see

Always asking what's Wrong

And my response is. . .

NOTHING!

I mean, we all know it's Something

But when I say Nothing

It's code for Leave it Alone

Drop it,

Or, Next Topic

O.M.G., you're still asking!

STOP IT.

My Mind is too Toxic!

I'm liable to Poison you
With the things Stained
To my Membrane.

You'll think I'm Insane
Cause my Mind is Unchained
Thank God that Down South
Right around my Mouth been Tamed

Cause the Brain ain't got No Filter
It's Raw, Unleashed, Released
Like a Rated R Matilda.

In my mind, I'm the Antagonist
Lurking for the Protagonist,
Yea, I'm the Villain
And I'm down for the Killing,
Chaos and Stealing.

In my Mind
I'm Drug Dealing
With a Thuggish Feeling
Oh Yea, I'm a Hard Body

I'm in the Driver Seat

But Passenger Side

Occupied

By the 12 Gauge Shotty!

I'm feeling like a Money-Making Mitch.

I ain't Paid in Full yet

So I'm liable to go, Rico,

She know,

I ain't down to be no Hero,

So my theme Music

Sound like Horror Flicks

Like Loki, I'm Mischievous

Full of Tricks

So I won't avenge her.

I said I'm like Loki

And on every Adventure

Never was he an Avenger.

See, y'all can't really Handle My Truth!

People ask for it

I mean, they beg for that Inner Bruce.

They Scream let him Loose

But the Bulk of My Hulk

Might change your Perspective of me

You may no longer be

Receptive of me

"This boy done lost his mind."

But the Thing is

I didn't Lose it

I just Removed it

But I forgot where I Left it.

But I'm sure wherever it is

Or around

Has now become Infected

Cause my Mind is beyond Septic

And Very Contagious

Leaking it's toxins into the closes eardrums

So Malicious.

And it smells so far past Death

The Buzzards won't even taste this

Who Lace this?

Brain with such Evil will

Once upon a time

There was such an even Keel

It was Innocent,

Stable, Rational, Just.

IDK what happened

But Imma just Blame Experience.

Drunk Dial

THAT'S CLEARLY IMPAIRED
YEA, I'M OFF THIS. . .
LIQUID COURAGE ON THE ROCKS
GOT ME STANDING TALL IN MY SOCKS

WATCHING TIME TICK
RIGHT AFTER IT TOCKS
GIRL I'M FUCKED UP.

Drunk Dial

Hey Shawty,
I know it's Late
But it COULDN'T WAIT
As I generate my Mental State

That's clearly Impaired
Yea, I'm off this. . .
Liquid courage on the Rocks
Got me Standing Tall in my Socks

Watching Time Tick
Right after it Tocks
Girl I'm Fucked up.
It's been a minute.
So really What's up!

Girl, don't act like that
Remember how this Wood
Used to Snap Yo Back

Knuckles and Hair Tangled
As I Wrap Yo Tracks
Then I Kiss Yo Tats

I'm tryna,

Smear the Ink.

Down between the Thighs

Where it's Colored Coded Pink.

Girl, it's real and you know

Tell me Baby, what you think.

I know you Fucking with the Vibe,

Baby Girl, we should Link.

And Vibe through Vibration

When I Arrive, Impatience,

Rush to me.

I long to see your body Yearn

Learn to Lust for me

Now I Love your Lust

But don't you Lie to me

Making Truth Hard to Trust

Until Ashes are Ashes

And Dust is Dust

Reincarnated

Just the 2 of us

You Hot and Ready

And I'm the Pizzas Crust

We both Edible

And eat til we Full

Reincarnated

Like Fools

We reused Tools

You nailed down with this Hammer

Caught Shawty in an Alley

When she OOOPED

I Slammed 'er

Lights on

No Camera,

But man, you Performing.

You got the wettest W.A.P.

It stay Storming

Heavy pouring

Ass out the Oven

That Warm, Gooey Loving

I'm Hypnotized

Caught between your Hips and Thighs

Pretty sure it's Ill-Advised

But I don't give a Fuck

She's my Pot of Gold

And I'm FULL of Beginners Luck

I love how you Strut,

With that Big Ole Butt

Nice tucked in Gut

A lady in the Street

Under-Sheet she Slut

So you Nasty Nasty

But Classy if you ask me

And Lastly

Where ya man at?

YOU CAN ALWAYS LEARN
SOMETIMES IN LIFE
IT JUST AIN'T YO TURN
BUT I PROMISE IT'S COMING

RIGHT WHEN TIMES ARE ROUGH
JUST DON'T GIVE UP
CAUSE ENOUGH IS NEVER ENOUGH!

Edification

Starring at the Top
From Down Below
Can be real Discouraging
Your Roots Planted
But won't Grow

And everything around you Flourishing
Man, I don't Understand
But I gotta thousand Excuses
Blame it on the devil and his Gang

Boy them demons Roofless
Sucking the Life out of me
Them demons Toothless.

Inside it Hurts my Pride
Cause I see 'em Looking Down
Until I learned that Top or Bottom
You're the Talk of the Town
Either way, Hating sounds
ALL-AROUND

Disguised as Encouragement

Poison they Feeding you

They calling it Nourishment

But careful the things you Digest

It may cause you to Digress,

But sometimes I Listen to the Noise and

I pick my Poison

Because those seem to be the Only Option

So when I see a man in a Bad Situation

I try to NEVER Knock Him

INSTEAD, Expound Wisdom

And find a way to Crop him

We could all use Growth

Your Friends and Enemies play a part

And we could all use both.

A Fall is better than a Stand Still

Because at least you Walked

And a few Bruises always Heal

But at least you Fought!

Done failed a few Test

But at least you thought

Exercise Yo Mental

Listen sometimes

Close your Dental

You can ALWAYS Learn

Sometimes in Life

It just AIN'T yo Turn

But I promise it's Coming

Right when times are Rough

Just Don't Give Up

Cause Enough is NEVER Enough!

Encouraging Words

> whatever you ask for in **prayer,** you shall receive if you believe.
>
> Mat 21:22

SO HAVE FAITH AND BELIEVE

ASKETH THE LORD

AND YE SHALL RECEIVE

HE WILL SUPPLY

ALL YOUR WANTS AND NEEDS

WITH HIM IN YOUR HEART

WHAT SATAN STOLE

WILL BE RETRIEVED

IT WAS NEVER HIS

DON'T BE DECEIVED

Encouraging Words

Stay strong in the Lord!
You CAN'T Erase the Past
But always Look Forward.

Your Goals,
Aim towards
Never STOP Striving!
Because not only God
But Satan is Arriving
To Kill, Steal, and Destroy!

Life is not a Game or Joke
He's after your Joy!

But No Weapon Formed Against You
Shall Prosper
Oh Father
Performs MIRACLES Every Day
That shocks doctors.

So HAVE FAITH and BELIEVE

Asketh the Lord

And ye shall Receive

He will supply

All Your Wants and Needs

With Him in your Heart

What Satan stole

Will be Retrieved

It was NEVER his

Don't Be Deceived.

Get thee,

Behind me

Satan!

On my knees

Til I find Peace

I'm Praying

Never Straying

Only Obeying

His Commanding Will
And His Outstanding Skills
Gives me a Demanding Thrill
To Overly Fulfill

God's Plan for me
My Destiny
My Spirit and Soul is there

But I gotta bring the rest of me
Cause my Stubborn Flesh

You See,
Sometimes gets the Best of me
And makes a Mess of me

Yes, Lord, I care
But moving Carelessly
And Lord it AIN'T Fair

Living Life like the Pharisees
My God
I gotta do better
Too smart for this
To Clever.

When Life is a Storm
Learn to Switch the Weather
When you're Pushed against the Wall
Learn to Pull it Together
Can't move like a Feather

In and out of the Wind
Constantly falling to Temptation
AND EVERY DAY SIN

God will Withhold
And Mold
Make Amends
And Cleanse

The Lord is my Shepherd

And He ALWAYS Defends

Even as I Offend

A Brother, my Mother, a Lover

Or Close Friend.

He provides Abundant Mercy

Again and Again

At times when I Lose

He's the Reason I Win

When I feel like a Zero

He's the One

That makes me feel like a Ten

Cause through it all

My Up's

And Downfalls

He was Right There by my Side

Through the Ugly Truth

That I Covered with Lies!

Lord, you are So Worthy

I don't deserve it

Yet, You keep showing Mercy

I'm down for Your Team Lord

Just Throw me a Jersey

And I'ma Grind til the Clock Stop

And I leave this Earth!

I could NEVER Live up to Your Son

But I GREATLY APPRECIATE His Worth!

Falling Leaf

A FALLEN LEAF ONLY PROGRESSION IS DOWNWARD
FLOWING IN ANY DIRECTION THE WIND CARRIES

Fallen Leaf

A **Fallen Leaf** only progression is Downward.

Flowing in any Direction the Wind Carries.

Wow! Such a Coward!

No Backbone to Stand Strong

But enough Pity to Lie Alone

You are your Worst Enemy

You are your own Clone!

Your Excuse is to Bring Joy

And NEVER Hurt Any Feelings

Tears soaking the Floor

As you look to the Ceiling

Once you were Full of Desire

Now you're NO LONGER Willing.

You've Lost All Passion

To your Positive Actions.

Now looking for Compassion

Cause you gave too much Attention

To all your Negative Distractions.

Fallen Leaf you're so Confused
You thought a Helping Hand
Was the devils Plan

So you Refused
Took the Road Mostly Traveled
For sure, you wouldn't Lose.

Did what you had to do
Abided by the Rules.

But the Whole Time
Being equipped with the Wrong Tools.
But I almost CAN'T Blame the Student
For what's being Taught in Today's Schools

It's a 50/50 Battle
It can go either way
But Right or Wrong Left or Right
In between its about 50 Shades of Grey

Such a SUBMISSIVE Mindset
To any Dominant Voice.
Had the option to Follow or Lead
And you Declined the Alpha Choice.

Seems to me you're SCARED to Fail!
But what if Ferdinand Magellan NEVER Sailed?!
Then this would be a Footnote in History
I wouldn't be allowed to tell!

So make a Lasting Impression
Leave Your Stamp.
Lead By Example
Be the Next Generation's Lamp.

Geometry

I have an Addiction

To our Addition!

We Make Love

On the Floor

Of our Sex-stained Kitchen.

I'm on Top

Next the Bottom

Constantly we Switching.

My angle 180 Degrees

I see it got you Twitching.

And as I Freelance

Standing taller than a Tree Branch

She tells me she CAN'T

"Daddy, you too deep."

But it's phrases like that,

Putting extensions on my Meat.

I Grind Harder

I'm taking Long Slow Strokes.

Your Moans are like Music to my Ears

How dare I MISS a Note.

If your body was Comedy

I understand EVERY Joke!

If your Personality was Gunja

Then I'm Chiefing Every Toat

I Love Yo Smoke!

Your beauty Stumbles Down

From ya Kinfolk!

You look just like your Mother

And if that's what I gotta look forward to for the next 30yrs

Then I'm Proud to call you my Lover

In Between, on Top, and Under the Cover

We making scenes, WON'T STOP

Satisfying each other

Girl, we make Kinetic Energy!

An Unbreakable Synergy.

You played hard to get
The Whole Time you was into me
If any Nigga has your Attention
Immediately he's my Enemy

You're more than just my Lover
Girl, you got a Friend in me
Now bend for me
Angle 90 Degree

I'll paddle your Sea
Faithfully,
Gratefully, and Graciously

Climax to Outer Space with me
Reaching Dimensions
Unleashing Sexual Tensions
Like 1st and 2nd Corinthians

You are my New Testament
I'm not a Soldier in this Game
Baby, I'ma Veteran

Yea, I got a Few Miles

I done been around the Block

Left to Right Flip Flop

While the Clock

Tick Tock

But I'm supplying Hard Rock

Like I just Pill Popped

Baby, I'm Ready,

But I'll take it Slow

We'll keep it Steady.

I want you up ALL NIGHT thinking of me

Till you Fall Asleep

Like I'm Freddy!

Every room you walk in

The airs Polluted with Confetti

You're my number 1 Trophy

And the way that you get Below me

Blow me,

On your Knees in such an Acute angle

Let's me know that you know me

Never been about too much Talking

You make an Effort to Show me.

You Lead by Example!

Confident I'd be Hooked

After your 1st Sample

Girl, You Brave!

And as I Surf your Wave

I'm so Enslaved

Your Whips, your Chains

You Pick my Brain

You Crave my Name

I'm Driven Insane

Apart from you

Can't Bear the Pain

SO HERE I COME!

Poetic Culture Vol. 1

Love Poem

YOUR EYES THE BRIGHT LIGHTS
TO MY DARKEST ROAD
YOU HELP ME STAY IN MY LANE
YES, I'M THE PILOT TO MY PLANE

BUT YOU ARE MY PROPELLER!
YOU HELP ME GET MY GROVE BACK
AS IF I WERE STELLA.

Love Poem

If I ever wrote a **Love Poem**
I guess it would Go
I mean, it would Flow
I really don't know

But something like this
Girl, every time we Kiss
I can feel your Breath
Grab My Heart
From the Darkest Abyss.

And it's Oh So Lovely
When you Hug me,

Cause your arms
Grab Hold of my Soul
Unraveling Stories Untold
Bringing Warmth
To what's Cold

Your eyes the Bright Lights

To my Darkest Road

You help me stay in my Lane

Yes, I'm the Pilot to my Plane

But you are my Propeller!

You help me get my Grove Back

As if I were Stella.

Y'all, she makes me Speak On Things

I said I would NEVER tell her!

And it wasn't by Force

Yet always by Choice,

And Oh how she Listens

Her Hearts Purer than Christians

On an Easter Sunday Morning

No Evil Will Intent!

And when my Pain

Is in the Louis Lane

She comes through

Like Clark Kent!

With a Capital S

On her Chest

Rest

And Assure

I can lay my Stress

Between her Breast!

She can handle

My Porcupine Flesh

Against her Armadillo Skin

You see she's Tough

A little Rough

A Niggas Charm WON'T Kill again

Her Hearts got one of its Senses Back

So It now can Feel again

Her Emotions Spill again

Forming a Circumference

Leaving us Stuck like Gilligan

But we will get off this Island

Cover all Corners

Squared off

Like We Tiling.

And if Pain is the Comedy

That keeps you Smiling

I'll Richard Pryor elbow open

In search for your Funny Bone.

I'm striving to be

A Worker Bee

In you Honey Zone

Your Honeycomb

I want no part of you unknown

You'll NEVER Stand Alone

As long as you Stand By my Side

The moment my Ignition starts

Need to know you Down to Ride.

No Element of Surprise!

I done did a lot of Lying

And been Lied too!

And if I'm being Honest

Can't say I'll NEVER Lie to you!

But if the Trigger Pulled,

Bullet out of the Barrel

I'll die for you!

If you Pull the Trigger

Bullet out of the Barrel

I'll Lie for you

You ask me to Jump

Dave Chapelle

How high for you

But if you wish to be apart

I won't say Goodbye for you

Because I'm selfish

Only if it ends with us ending together

Will I be selfless

Cause our Love

You can't Shelf this

It's Priceless, Rare,

Never found in stores,

It's Righteous and I'm Aware

That it's earned through Chores

Relationship Chores,

I'll do my part

If you Promise to do yours.

If I outlive you

Rest In Peace

Here take my Peace with you

Sometimes I Truly Believe

Heaven Above Sent YOU

Then again,

Sometimes I feel

Like you're from the Depths of the Sea

But you're my Sour Patch

So it really DON'T bother me

Make a Father of me

Bring Forth the Sons

And Daughters in me!

Oh, how the Wifely Mother Role

Wears on you

The Light

From the Mirror of Emotions

Glares on you

You Wear your Heart upon your Sleeves

Your Pride Tucked Inside

Between Yo Thighs

Above Yo Knees

You are a Real Woman

Not just anyone

Can Bare your Fruit

When it's Cumming!

You taught me something!

The Lust between our Love

Keeps us Wet

When we Dry Humping

You know that part

When I make you feel

Like ya Thighs Numbing

When the Climax

Climaxes

You Open up your Heart

And Dangerous Love Surpasses

Into a place

Where you said for the Longest

No Trespassing

And I'm not Gassing

But,

I noticed your Fuel was Low.

And now that I have your Heart on Go

Your Mind still pumps the Brakes

Cause nowadays

Not much to take

For your Earth to Quake

Your Milk to Shake

You need Stability

The 1st and 2nd didn't work

But I don't Plan to be a Trilogy

I wanna be your King

A title well deserved

From the words

Of my Queen.

How bout we be a team,

And Plot against the World

You're my Temptation

I'm David Ruffin

When I speak on "My Girl"

Sunshine on the Cloudiest Day

If it ain't yo feelings

I don't give a Fuck

Who Rains on our Parade,

Cause the Sun still Shine

And Baby Girl

You still fine

And through all the Bullshit

Baby girl, you still mine

I get Lost in your Love

As if you Steal Time

We Coexist together

Like Rhythm and Rhyme

Needles and Pine

Wind and Chimes

Big Boobs

And alotta Behind

We just match

Addicted to your Heroine Love

Gives me that Junkie Scratch

Won't be Detached

Cause I'll suffer from Withdrawals

I drop my Three Hoes

I'm done being Santa Claus

Coming down every Chimney

Didn't make a man at all

But you Bring out the Best in Me

You invest in me

And through all the Bull

You Never the Less in me

You NEVER doubted

Even though I gave Reason

Because the Act of Betraying you

Is the Definition of Treason

Masquerade

Our relationships Platonic

We Dance, We Drink

Smoke a Lil Chronic

Short Shorts, Tank Top

No Bra and a Bonnet

We just Netflix and Chill

Still to this day

She picks the best Flicks for real

Suspense that's a lil' Intense

Mixed with a Love Story

Her Favorite Category

We both order Habachi

In our matching Hurachaes

What!!!

That's our thing!

Matching Monday.

Go-carts, Mini-golf, Funnel cakes

What a Fun Day

We party hard on the weekend
And praise em harder on Sunday
And she about her business too.

She Grinds for a Dollar
Then Finesse it into two
She gotta son by a low life
Saved in her Phone as Issue
And as usual

Right after being called a Bitch
Issue Blurts out
I miss you
And the Water Streaming
Into the Tissue

Soon Dries
I've always Admired your Strength
But I've watched you Weaken
To those Lies

You drive a Dangerous Path
Ignoring all the Road Signs

Yolo!

A phrase your actions portray at times

You Wild Girl.

I mean like

Wow Girl!

You One of a Kind.

Thinking of this while we Chill

Like is it worth Crossing the Line

Am I wasting my

Fuck it!

I gotta make you Mine.

No, No, No, No,

As I struggle inside

Words on the tip of my Tongue

Tied down by my pride.

The moment I agreed to this Friendship

I lied,

Cause,

I've been in Love with you.

My Addiction

My Addiction causes an affliction

That gets down in my soul

I ain't gone front

Be I've been told

That I can't control

What I won't confront.

Bad habits that I've formed

Were never reborn

They were just generational curses

That's cursing louder than ever

Standing in my pops chair

With my grandfather's noose

Around my neck

Thinking I'm getting better

So prideful of **My Addiction**

I'm ashamed to say the 1st letter

I observed the example put before me

And I said that I would never!

But yet, here I am

Dealing with a Familiar Struggle

My Spirit Screaming on the inside

But my flesh is Strapped with a Muzzle

Mind Scrambled in a Thousand Pieces

With no way to put back the Puzzle

Enough words, but not enough time

Like a game of Ruzzle!

Cause I mean what I don't say

And say what I don't mean

My words start to Rebuttal

My Addiction is so Subtle

When my Loved ones reach out for **my Addiction**

I form Anger, Embarrassment,

And Prideful Tension.

Pretty sure that was the moment

Where I should've Listened,

Naw. . .

To worried about the next Fix in'

Sometimes I can't believe myself
Keep calling myself a Christian

I am,
But it's one Hell of a devil mixed in
Lord bring 'em out!
Let my Prayers turn into Worship
As I begin to Shout!

I Need You Father,
YOU ARE SO WORTHY!

I Need You Father,
YOU'RE UNDYING MERCY!

I NEED YOU FATHER!
I NEED YOU FATHER!

Poetic Culture Vol. 1
On My Mind

ROSES ARE RED
BUT THAT AIN'T ALWAYS TRUE
I READ BETWEEN THE LINES OF MY BIBLE
AS I SIP THE DEVILS JUICE
SO MUCH ON MY MIND
I'VE BECOME IDLE WITH TIME

On My Mind

Roses are Red

But that AIN'T ALWAYS True

I read between the Lines of my Bible

As I sip the devils' Juice

So much **on my mind**

I've become Idle with time

On the Brink of Depression

Resting turns into Stressing

Life's a Hard Lesson

Yet my Heart is still Guessing

She Loves Me

Or She Loves Me NOT

My Destination is your Heart

So, provide me with Options

For that is the only way I can Choose

And if you Refuse

I'll try again NOT to Lose

But help me Win.

I Chase after the Thoughts

In your mind

But you keep moving the Finish Line

It's hard to read your Body Language

And that causes Mental Anguish

Between my temples!

When I don't notice the smile

Between yo dimples,

It causes me to wonder

Cause your smile is lighting striking

And your laugh is roaring thunder.

You make me feel surrounded

My love, your lust compounded

Now my feelings all in it

But your emotions still pending

At times I don't get you,

And you claim you don't get flu

But I seem to be the symptoms

That make you sick

Just a sip of my liquor

Got you lit

Are we not meant to coexist

Am I not the equation

To your find a man list

Baby talk to me.

Your eyes are screaming

But your mouth won't say a word

Your touch is numb

Your mind a caged bird

Your ears clipped wings

Tongue deadly and sharp

Like bee stings

But I won't have an allergic reaction.

The subtraction of your Heart

Minus the retraction of your body

Causes a contraction in my soul

And I feel it growing cold

But my attitude is heated
I know I can't force your love
But my feet are defeated
Bare footed
I walked loose gravel roads for you
Till the point they bleeded
I meant bled
No I really meant still bleeding
I'm sending you all types of effort
But you still not receiving.

So I'm big mad at you now
I ain't got Nothing to say
Hold up! Wait!
I already miss you
You're always on my mind
Getting you off
Seems to be the issue.

Reminiscing

I **reminisce** on the times

That we had together.

The Shallows and the Highs

But we Persevered through the Weather.

When it seemed as if

the struggle wasn't getting any better,

you showed me tough love

Said that's enough! So rub

your eyes and stop crying

I'm your mom and I'm trying!

To do the best I can.

To draw up a plan

on how to teach from a woman's point of view

How to be a man.

Strong words from a dying woman.

Her death was like a snake in high grass

I didn't even see it coming!

Because when she worked

she grinded,

if she searched

she would find it.

The way she lived!

It was to the upmost,

and when she danced

it was for our Father the Holy Ghost.

What a role model

to follow and frame after

Tammy Brown is her Name

and I'll continue to right her chapter.

I'm her legacy that lives on

She's my pedigree that's long gone

But I keep her close to home

Like a front yard Nome

Or a gun in its holster

That hasn't yet been drawn!

See now when I **reminisce**

I remember this

Momma always told me

Son ignorance is bliss

so don't rely on athleticism

And get your education in the midst.

Then with two hands

she grabs my forehead and softly kiss

her gentle touch

I truly miss

Oh the times I **reminisce**.

Together we had so much fun

I couldn't ask for a better bond

between a mother and her son.

When I lost her

It seemed like my world was coming to an end

Y'all she wasn't just my mother

She was my best friend

Closer than 9 is to 10

Or two identical twins.

Mom I miss you!
And my only issue
seems to be
the lack of tissue
when the tears flow from my eye to the floor
rapidly like a missile!

August 5, 2008
it's the day it became official
I lost you forever
but your words will always remain
Momma I hope I'm making you proud
until that day we meet up again!

Role Model Father

It's 3 a.m. and he Stumbles in
He said he'd be home 5 hours ago
Sometime around 10.

Momma's mad as Hell!
Yelling, "Where have you been?"
She's ready for War,
But this Battle she won't Win.

He's Drunk and out of his Mind,
Beating my mother Senseless!
He does it all the Time!
She's Hurt, Body Bruised.

Claiming it was a Fall.
Little did she know last night I heard it all

Even pops Apology,
"Come on Bae it's the Alcohol.
You know how I get when I Drink
Just reacting to the Situation
I don't even think."

His mouth is like a Record,

Constantly on Repeat.

Cause the next night I witnessed

What I didn't wanna See!

My mother upside down,

Dangling from her feet.

As she screams, "No, Stop!

Please let go of me."

My eyes are Wide,

I can't believe my View.

Stuck I can't Move,

What's a young fella supposed to do?!

Scared and Upset

I just ran to my Room.

Slammed the Door Shut,

All you could Hear was a loud BOOM!!!

Next my dad comes in

Loud & Energetic.

Saying boy if you don't come from Under that Bed

You'll regret it!

While mothers saying son it's Alright,

Everything's Copacetic.

But what I just saw

I'll NEVER Forget it.

A child Witnessing Adult Drama,

I got a Heart Full of Fear,

Feeling Traumatized!

Momma Crying!

Daddy say Shut Up

She say I'm trying

But you Scaring my son

You scaring what's Mine!

Pop said what the Fuck!!!

Shit he mine too!

I was the One

That put that Seed inside you.

Now they're Back & Forth Fussing
Momma Yelling, Daddy Cussing!

I close my Eyes and Cover my Ears
To disappear from what appears
To be a Heated Discussion.

Until I heard a Loud Smack
I quickly looked Back
Thinking When, Who, Where,
What the Hell was that?!

Damn!
Again Mothers Under Attack!
Man, this Shit is Wack!
But I remain to be Intact,
Through all this Commotion

In My Mind,
I escape to the Ocean,
Because in my Fantasy,
That's the Life I've Chosen

Life is Sweet,

Everything's Golden!

Pops DON'T Drink,

And Momma Lip ain't Swollen.

But then I Snap Back to Reality,

Where I resume Watching a Fatal Casualty.

He Beats her

And continues to Beat her

Then he Chokes her

Till she Loses her Breath

I knew what I saw wasn't Right

But the Coward in me

Just made me Turn Left

While I Listen to my mother Scream

As she Faces Death!

But then there was a Sudden Silence

The final outcome of Domestic Violence.

My mother laying there Dead

Dads Panicking,

And he says

"Baby, wake up!
You heard what I said.
I didn't mean for this to happen
I just lost my Head."

Boom! Boom! Boom!
Open up it's the Feds!
Pop went from Sad to Mad
Eyes Bloodshot Red.

Went and got his Gun,
And filled the clip Full of Lead.
He looked at me, said,
"Shhh don't you come from under that bed."

Once he opened the Door
I hear words Exchange,
But Pops story ain't adding up
Cops looking at him Strange.

As if he were Deranged
Cops just said

"Hold up, Sir!

Let me first get your Name."

Pops, now getting Impatient,

He knows they not Buying the story he Selling

And after tonight's Crime

He's sure to be a Felon

And 12 ain't Caught up

In all the Lies he Telling.

Now back to me up under the bedsprings,

I finally grow some nuts!

Help! Help! To the Top of my Lungs I Scream

I Dealt, but yet I Melt

To the Background that I have seen!

Not good for my Health,

So I Wept,

Over the Breakdown,

I'm in between!

Losing my Mind

And Losing my Voice.

Feds rush in,
Because they have no other choice.

They Bum Rush my father,
I hear him Sarcastically Laughing,
They come in
Pull me from under the bed and said,
"Son, tell us what happened!"

Same Ole Story

Same Ole Story,
Is he ever gone Change?
His Actions beg for Attention,
Or some Sort of Fame.
He feels Desperate and Lonely,
So he Joins a Gang.

Doing any and everything they ask
Just for Recognition to his Name.
Now he's Wilding Out,
He can't be Tamed.

Screaming and Shouting to the top of his Lungs,
"I'll ride or die for the game!"

Aww man, what a Shame,
His mind is Clouded with Confusion,
And little did he know,
A Bullet would be his Conclusion.

But it's the **Same Ole Story,**

We've heard it all before,

He even saw the Signs,

But he decided to Ignore.

He said, "Naw!!! Not my niggas,

They wouldn't bust through the Door,

Put a Gun to my Head

And Force me to the Floor.

Naw Not Me!

You See!

I was to Loyal!"

Now a mother has to watch her Son

Be put in the Soil.

Because he wouldn't Smarten up,

He was so Naive

And now he can't believe,

The ones he called Brothers

Are beating him till he Bleeds,

To the point that he Dry Heaves.

You see,

I show Empathy,

Because I understand his Situation,

But I don't show Sympathy,

He should've made some Mental Alterations!

But Oh, how Amazing!

The Power of Persuasion.

He had so much Truth,

Lying in False Accusations!

Now he can't Watch his Seed Grow,

You know!

The Next Generation.

Like Father, Like Son,

What a Bad Imitation!

Sad to say,

He won't make it to his Graduation.

But it's the **Same Ole Story**,

Just a different Chapter!

Like a Camera when Snaps,

One Pose is all it Captures.

Silver Lining

I fell asleep last night
Thinking bout the Good Times
We used to Blow two L's
Beginning to Unwind
From a Stressful Day
You Vocalize your Mind
I pour a glass of Bubbly for two
Of that Fine Wine.

I would Observe as you Sip
Thinking you're mine
I only had Two Nickels to my Name
Still you wanted to be my Dime!

You ordered me two chains
Supported my Dream
I was Extremely Blessed!

Y'all ain't get that
I said she ordered me 2 chainz
Supported my Dream
I was Extremely Blessed!

Extremely blessed! Ahhh-ah-ah-ah
But yea I said was,
Because,
It's the Present Day Past.

Thought we had that kinda Love
That would Buzz Light Year Last!
To Infinity and Beyond

Girl, I thought you were for me
When did our Relationship
Form a Toy Story

You go from your Past towards
Your Present Presence
Fast Forwards
Into your Future.

But let me help you Rewind
Relapse, Jog your Memory
I'm talking Remind
Reminisce on the Times
Of the fine Wine & Dinner Dines

Girl, I miss you!

How did this happen?

What was our Issue?!

Was it me

That made you Flea?!

Did I not Follow the Steps

Like A B C

1 2 3

D E F G

4 5 6

Girl, I'm torn to Bits

Bout to have a Fit

And I won't Quit

Until, I'm surrounded by your Voice

Stimulated by your Hands

Caressed between your right to Left Thigh

Introduced and Seduced

To your Sexual Mile High

You're the Wind Beneath my Wings

Which causes me to Fly

Reaching elements above the Sky

For you I'll try

Until the day I Die

To many nights I would cry

Wondering why

Blinded by Tears

But now my eyes are Dry

I'm after your Location

I scheduled a Netflix reservation

And I hope can you make it

Any answer but Yes

Don't think I can take it

I know you still Love me

I just wanna hear you say it.

Don't let your mind Delay it

Let it Catch up with your Heart

I know you miss our Fire Sparks

Don't tell me I'm Wrong,

Don't leave me Alone

Cause an Idol Mind

Is the devils workshop

And I'm starting to Feel

Like I'm too Far Gone

Baby pick up the Phone

Stop sending me to Voicemail

But if that's the only way

I can hear your Voice, well!

I guess that's my **Silver Lining**!

Subconscious

Please let me Explain

This Excruciating Pain

Inside of me

There's a Burning Wildfire Flame

That can't be Tamed

Even in the Midst

Of pouring down Rain

I stay Clouded

Full of Shame

The Hurt is so Deep

But I Compress it within my Veins

The Secrets I Keep

Internally Killing me

Externally I Weep

Yes, the Inner me is Dying

While the Enemy grooms a Lonely Cub

Into a Depressed Mountain Lion

But I keep a Smile upon my Face
To avoid myself from Crying
Telling others I'm Alright
Constantly I'm Lying

Resorting to Drugs and Alcohol
Two things I've become Reliant
Of mixing the two
Deadly science
The more I'm influenced to Slow Down
The more I become Defiant.

Something is Screaming on the inside of me
It won't be Silent!
Feels like I'm in a Plane that's Collapsing
Turns out I'm the Pilot.

Or a Sunken Ship
And I'm the Captain
Wondering where I went wrong?
Confused on really what happened!
Enough Tears to Replenish the Sea
But never enough Napkins!

Not a Shoulder to Cry On
Or a Penny for my Thoughts,
My Life is an Open Flesh Wound
Encouraging Words feel like Salt!

I don't know who to Trust
Starting to feel like the First Man
Made from Dust!

I fall into Sin
And I become Weak
Forgot to be a Man
And Stand on my own Two Feet

I feel Pain, Suffering,
And Overwhelming Defeat
Stuck in this Phase of Life
I'm on Repeat.

Trapped in my Mental
Only Escape Route
Through the Dental!

But I find it hard to Express My Heart

Because the moment I do

Here comes Cupid with Poisonous Darts

Arrows of Rats, Foxes, and Snakes

In other words

Full of Snitches, Liars, and Fakes

Tsunamis, Tornadoes, and Earthquakes

My Life is a Wreck

But I was the Driver

I chose this Path

And became the Only Survivor

Lost Loved Ones and Enemies

Bad Decisions are my Tendencies

When will I EVER Learn?

It's like when Evil comes around

I wait on my Turn.

I know the Fire is Hot

But I choose to get Burned

Oversleeping on my Blessing
Knowing the Early Bird Gets the Worm
I hope one day Soon
I learned my Lesson

Before my mouth can't Contain
These hidden Confessions
And my Body Weakening
From the Lack of NEVER Resting

Because I am the Pen
And Life I Continue Testing!
So far,
I'm Failing

The Difference between Me and You

The difference between me and you
Is like the **difference** between a Cold and the Flu
Like the **difference** between a Farm and a Zoo

You see!
I'm not Knocking what you do
I'm just on a different Type of Mission
While you Hunting for Bass,
I'm hunting for Sharks when we Fishing

Listen!
While you're Living for the Now,
I'm preparing for the Later
I Plot, Plan, and Scheme
Only to be Greater.

A Wise Man once told me
"If you don't plan, you plan to fail.
So stay the Course son
And NEVER Derail."

Those were Wise Words
From a Man of Intelligence
I took it and Ran!

Haven't looked back ever since
But that's the difference between you and I
I was given Wings and Headed for the Sky,
But NEVER did I skip the Process
Of Learning how to Fly.

See while you were feeling Unsure
I was Confident
I feel that any Obstacle coming my way
Through God, I can Conquer it
Emotional, Spiritual, or Financial,
He'll sponsor it!

I know what I am,
I'm an Imperfect Christian
You, on the other hand,
Seems to be a Little Blurred on your Mission

But I use the Holy Bible to clear up my Vision

Because Faith + Praise = BLESSINGS

Simple addition

But you!

Trying to make it WITHOUT God

Complicated Division

Tomorrow

I'ma Villain in most stories

But like most Plots

With Deep Thoughts

I had good Intentions

Labeled Bad, Evil

You see,

Good was NEVER mentioned

Alotta built-up Tension

And women,

Were just Stress Relievers

Sorta like my Aspirin

Can I come Chill

Just asking

Never wanted all off one

Just a Fraction

But what does that say about me

Selfish, Inconsiderate.

If women an Open Book

Then I must be Illiterate

Cause I can't get past the 3rd Chapter

My ill will could Care Less bout what's after

And what makes it Badder

I mean really makes me Madder

Is that she Thicker than Webster

Smarter than Dexter

Man, what a Combo

And every time I Fuck up

All I can say is ION know

It's started Off Good

Shit, where did the time go?

When it Rains, it Pours

Plus Time Slow

All the Good Times a Blur

Just ask Pop

He ain't Popped Champagne

Since Kawahi was a Spur

So enjoy the Sunshine

While the Sun Shining Bright

Cause that Darkness Creeps
All through the Night
And all through the Light

The Moon NEVER goes away
So careful what enters your ear Gate
Cause we walking Round on Ground
Where demons Pray
And the devil Play.

He'll have you Stressed out bout **Tomorrow**
But enjoy today
Cause just like Yesterday
Tomorrow's NOT Promised to you.

Trial & Error

I do what I do

Because I can

Ima Black African

American

With a Dark tan

My mistakes and Accomplishments

Made me this Man

And I won't Stand

For no more Bullshit!

Whether it be from a Friend or Foe

Or the Man in the Pulpit!

Don't tell me what I gotta Right to Feel

If I'm on the Hunt

Don't tell me what I gotta Right to Kill

I'll Trap, Trace, and Erase My Meal

Got enough Cap Space
In this place
To Display my Skills!

My Stubborn Will
Just won't let me quit
Until I find my Niche.

I'm angrily Motivated
Passionately Dedicated
For my family
Who never made it
Ima Break and Recreate the Cycle!

I will make a difference,
It's hard at times
Feels like I can't cover the Distance
Like I'm trying to move Lateral
With a Torn Meniscus

What is this!

Only I can fix this

2.0 remix this

Mind my own business

And stay on my grind

I don't care if you judge my past

That's how I'm defined

Through the mountains I've climbed

With a devilish mind

Lord forgive me!

For I have Sinned

Relapse to my Old Ways

Back in the Old Days

Now has become a Trend!

If I keep Falling

How can I Lead Men

Make the Odds Even

So many Stumbling Blocks

But what's the Reason!

Trial and Error

Trust the Process

See

It wasn't that my Dreams

DIDN'T MATTER

My self-esteem just Shattered

I listened to all the Haters' Chatter

And I was the next up Batter!

But now

When I Step to the Plate

I'm hitting Home Runs

I'm Daddy now

But I started off a Son

Had to be Taught to

Crawl, Walk, then Run

Still a Work in Progress

When it comes to the Flying Part

I'm still Mapping out the Blueprints

When it comes to Defining my Art!

But in order for me to be Understood

I had to 1st Understand

Needed to be a Boy

To Desire being a Man

It's the Doubt that you can't

Motivates that you can.

Lebron took his Talents to South Beach

Then he Brought One to the Land

Trust the Process!

Joel Embid

Philadelphia 76ers

The best Center in the League.

Letters, Words, to Sentence

How I learned to Read.

Following Negative & Positive Influences

The way I Learned to Lead.

Because of that
Gives you the King
That Stands within your Presence.

Growing up
Didn't have the Courage to say that
I was Rooted Amongst the Peasants.

But when I make it,
Yes! I'm gone make it!
I gotta bring my People.

The ones that Watered my Roots,
And helped me reach my Highest Steeple.

And for the Haters on my Roots,
Thank you for the Fertilizer.
Y'all never saw my Future Down the Road
To busy Observing the Student Driver!

So, if you ain't Rocking with me now

Then Rock-a-Bye Nigga

I'm on my R Kelly Version

Believing I can Fly Nigga

Before my time come

I Plan to die Richer!

From a Penny

To a Nickel,

Nickel in two,

A Dime,

Dime into a Quarter,

Quarter into a Dollar.

Hustling's in my Blood

School of Hard Knocks

Where I became a Scholar

The Times that my Father

Grabbed me by the Collar

And said,

"See, you was supposed to Break the Cycle."

And I'ma help you do it

You was Programmed with all the Pieces

And I'ma help you Glue it

Standing over you while you Eat your Veggies

Making sure that you Chew it!

My plan is to tell you Twenty Years from now

"Son! I already knew you could do it."

Thanks, Pop!

Because of him

For Good and Bad

I don't Mind the Struggle

It Turned me into a Survivor.

But I don't just wanna Survive

I wanna Live

I'm like Chris Rock when I Arrive

I only got Enough for one Rib.

I just ain't got it like that

If y'all understand what I'm saying

But I'ma Keep Working,

Keep Grinding

And most of all, keep Praying

TRUST THE PROCESS!

Uprooted Against My Will

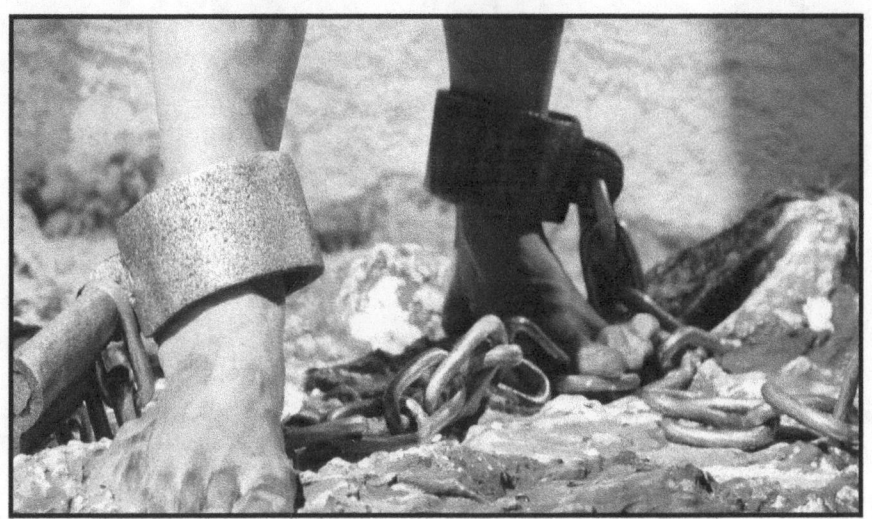

DIED A SLAVE,
BUT I WAS BORN FREE.
TOLD I WASN'T WORTH MORE
THAN THE SHACKLES ON MY FEET.

Uprooted Against My Will

Died a Slave,

But I was Born Free.

Told I wasn't Worth more

Than the Shackles on my Feet.

Purchased with Chains on my Hands

By an Unfamiliar White Man

Sold by an Ignorant Degenerate

Who shared my same Color Pigment.

They Forced me upon a Boat

And Traveled into a New World

They immediately broke my Spirit

And instantly Fucked my girl.

I was Thrown in the Fields

And was Given a Name.

I Complied; I NEVER Lied!

Yessir Massa!

Completely Trained.

And never get caught

Enhancing your Medulla Oblongata

Caucasian man saw African girl Reading,

And urgently he Shot her!

Days upon Days

I ponder about my Freedom.

But I watched a man Escape for his

And to the Death they Fiercely Beat Him.

He was made an EXAMPLE

For all the Rest!

They Hung his Body from a Neuse

His Cadaver!

Unrecognizable Flesh.

How Unfair!

To be Uprooted against my will,

To be Forced to Stand,

But allowed to Kneel.

How Unfair!

To be uprooted against my will,

Every day I watch my own People

Get Raped, Tortured, and Killed!

But it's everyday Life.

It's become a Normalcy!

African Kings hanging from Trees!

African Queens please Massa Needs!

Has truly become a Reality.

As a People,

Where the Fuck did we go WRONG?!

Was it Education?! Slight Hesitation?!

It remains to be Unknown.

But NO LONGER will I

Play the Victim Role.

I Pray to the Sky

Hoping that He hears my Soul

I refuse to Cry!

Because my Heart is Cold!

Grounded! Rooted!
No more against my will.

Our Forefathers Were Founded
But Alluded!
To the Songs, they Sung in the Fields!
UPROOTED AGAINST OUR WILL!

What She Can't Have

She's Crying,

All in her Feelings!

Because of some man

She was Sexually Dealing With!

You see,

The Truth was always a Myth!

Let me help y'all understand.

From day 1 she already knew the Plan

But she Fucked Up

When she tried to make him her Man.

Everything was Cool

They had a Smooth System,

Until she replaced her Mind with her Heart.

In other words, she LOST her Wisdom.

Now she Weeping to her Homegirls,

That she Miss 'em, wanna Kiss 'em

Because so Desperately

She wants what she can't have,

She's trynna Comprehend

What she CAN'T, Grasp!

She knew from the Start,

That the End WOULDN'T Last.

But the more she saw a Future with him

His presence begin to Pass.

But the Past is where she remains.

Him & Her, Her & Him

Is what's stained to her Brain.

Willing to do anything

For the Rights to his Last Name,

But Shawty you already knew the Game!

You was Dealing with a Dog off his Leash

You knew he couldn't be Tamed!

Determined to make him

The match to your Flame

The Nova to your Cane

Because like a Drug
You were Addicted
Now going through withdrawals
Trynna find a way to Kick it

Your Mind, Body, and Soul
Broken and Conflicted
Troubled and Afflicted
Only thing you wanna do now
Is redial his Seven Digits.

Because so Desperately
She wants what she can't have
Steadily trynna touch
What she can't Grab!

Now she's Venting,
Crying out her Eyes.
But as the Tears Flow,
It still wouldn't Drown away the Lies
She's wondering how she Ends up
With these type of guys.

She tells her Homegirl
"I try not to let it phase me."
But it's really starting to Amaze me.

I can't believe I Fell for it again,
To these Lazy No Good Boys,
Who call themselves Men!

I'm beginning to see the Trend
They Fuck you and LEAVE
But still wanna remain Friends,

As time goes by,
Now they trynna make Amends!

I was Blinded
But now I see Perfectly
Through this one-sided Lenses."

No longer will she Allow a boy
To take away her Joy,
Play with her Heart,
Toss it to the side like a Toy.

Because no longer will she Strive

For what she can't have!

Now pulling out the Knife in her back

From where she's been Stabbed!

Patching up a Wound

That continues to Bleed.

Now using the Word of God

To Sufficiently Supply her Needs!

Zurita Murphy

I got this Bad Lil Thang
Go by the Name of **Zurita**.
I bring the Wine, she order Pizza,
And she fine while she rolling Reefer.

A Lil Hood, with a lot a Diva,
Misunderstood to a lot a people.
Angel like, with the Kiss of Evil
Beauty blinding
She's so Deceitful.

Mesmerizing got me Diamond Sizing
The thought of you Leaving is Traumatizing.

Our Love and Lust
Staircase arising
She broke my Trust
Well, that ain't surprising.

That's the devil's daughter.
Here to Kill, Steal, and Destroy
In that order.

At times I call her Demon Semon

Nightmare on Hell Street

She crack a Smile when she Dreaming.

Things far fetched

She really had me Believing.

She was O.D.D.

So, she had to get even.

Just her Presence

They Retrieving.

Shawty temp off the scale

All she needed was a reason.

A Savage in her own right,

And when I comes to a Fight

She on site

Defending hers.

No matter what she Heard

Know her Bond is her Word.

So, she Bending All Curves,

But NEVER Cutting ANY Corners.

She about her Money and Love to Fuck

Shit that's a BONUS.

Nails clean

But her hands get Dirty.

Knows exactly what she wants

Even though she's a Lil Flirty

Lil Country in me,

Let her know she Purty.

I'm bout to be 29

And she pushing 30

So, we got Plenty Time

We ain't in a hurry.

Just me and ZURITA MURPHY.

ABOUT THE AUTHOR

ISAAC BROWN JR.

I was born May 21, 1992, in Frankfort, Germany. The reason is that my father was a soldier in the U.S. Army. I was only there after my birth for approximately two years, then my parents and I headed for the States.

As I began to age, basketball became my favorite pastime. At times, I felt as if I loved the game more than it loved me; I still persevered through trial and error, and I now withhold memories, moments, mistakes, and accomplishments from the game that I share with young men and women. Hopefully, my past will make brighter futures for the young minds I instill.

Poetry is my second favorite pastime, right after basketball. I always took an interest in rhythm, rhyme, and patterns, but I never did pick up a pen and start writing until 2008, when my mother passed away. I did not know I had it in me, but for some reason, that is the only way my mind would release negative energy. I could not stop writing once I started, and I have not looked back since. **"Where is She"** is the first poem I ever wrote. I cried as I wrote the piece, only thinking of my deceased mother, but little did I know the power of poetry rose within me.

Image References

http://wildernessinnovation.com/

https://cherigamble.com/

https://www.fg-a.com/

https://um-insight.net/

https://wol.jw.org/

https://i.ytimg.com/

https://www.indiamart.com/

https://www.wbur.org/

https://christiancounselingco.com/dont-give-up-you-can-do-this/

https://www.freeiconspng.com/

https://www.zastavki.com/pictures/originals/2014/Aviation_Propeller_plane_079288_.jpg

www.ingramcontent.com/pod-product-compliance
Lightning Source LLC
Chambersburg PA
CBHW011406070526
44577CB00003B/391